GODFREY TEMPLE

ATTENTION FACTORY

The Essential Guide on How to Determine What Deserves Your Attention, Learn How to Determine Priorities and Focus on the Right Things in Your Life

Descrierea CIP a Bibliotecii Naţionale a României
GODFREY TEMPLE
ATTENTION FACTORY. The Essential Guide on How to Determine What Deserves Your Attention, Learn How to Determine Priorities and Focus on the Right Things in Your Life / Godfrey Temple – Bucharest: Editura My Ebook, 2021
ISBN

GODFREY TEMPLE

ATTENTION FACTORY

The Essential Guide on How to Determine What Deserves Your Attention, Learn How to Determine Priorities and Focus on the Right Things in Your Life

My Ebook Publishing House
Bucharest, 2021

TABLE OF CONTENTS

FOREWORD

There are plenty of things in life that probably affect the way you make decisions, and different things which can grab your interest every now and then. However, the truth is, not everything in life really deserves your attention. There are instances when you simply need to let go of some things and divert your attention to those that are more important and urgent, those that really matter. In this book, hopefully, you will get to learn how to be disciplined enough in order for you to pinpoint those things that really deserve your attention and the ones that you simply need to forget.

What Deserves Your Attention

CHAPTER 1

DISCIPLINE BASICS

Synopsis

What is discipline all about? How can you say that you are truly disciplined enough? Being disciplined is more than knowing what you should and should not do and there are still many things that you should know about this "D" word.

Discipline – What Is It All About?

Discipline is a behavioral pattern where you are the one who chooses to do the things that you know should be done instead of those that you want to do. Discipline is the inner power pushing you to get out of your bed to exercise every morning instead of sleeping for extended hours. It is when you assert your willpower over the basic desires that you have. Discipline is in fact synonymous with self-control.

When you are disciplined, you have the personal initiative of getting started together with the stamina to carry on. When you are disciplined, you will have the strength of withstanding difficulties and hardships, whether they are physical, mental or emotional. This allows you to forgo immediate satisfaction so that you can achieve something better, even it calls for time and effort.

Needless to say, discipline is among the cornerstones in order to live a fulfilling and successful life, something that everyone, including you, should try to master.

The Perks of Being a Disciplined Person

Once you are consistently doing things that you know you need to do exactly when you know that you should be doing them, there are several benefits that you can enjoy:

- You are going to achieve your goals. Once you are consistently doing things that you know should be done, you are also increasing your chances of attaining your goals.

- Other people's respect for you will also grow, which will include your spouse, your employee and those who can witness all your efforts.

- Your self-esteem is going to soar. Each time you push yourself into doing things that you know should be done, your self-esteem is going to build up.

- You can influence other people's lives. All the right and good things that you do can influence other's lives who are watching, which can have a ripple effect on the future generations.

- You are going to witness greater success in the different facets of your life.

- The last but not the least, your life will be more satisfying and rewarding when you are disciplined.

The Downsides of Not Being Disciplined

If you are consistently neglecting the things that you know you should do when they need to be done, there are downsides that you can expect for:

- You will never be able to meet your goals.

- You will never feel great about yourself even if you try hard in justifying your actions.

- You are going to lose the respect of the people who depend on your actions.

Choosing to become a disciplined person can actually be considered as one of the most crucial decisions that you will ever make in your life, all because of the undeniable fact that this holds a powerful influence on practically all areas of your life.

CHAPTER 2

TREATING OTHERS
WITH LOVE AND RESPECT

Synopsis

Love and respect comes two-fold. You cannot be harsh to other people and disregard their feelings and expect them to still look at you with adoring and considerate eyes. Learn the true importance of respecting and loving the people around you and how it can change the way they treat you as well.

Respect and Love Others For Them To Do The Same To You

In all kinds of relationship, romantic or not, the combination of love and respect is actually the real secret in order to make things last.

For some reason, some people today often confuse respect with fear. There are gangs that fight and kill for respect but instead, they create fear among other people. Domestic abusers beat their partners and demand for respect but then again, fear is all they got, not respect.

But respect is not something that you get out of hurting others. It is not something that you achieve by just demanding others to give it to you. You do not impose respect, you earn it.

In the same way that you want to be respected, it is important that you also start to learn respecting other people. Whether it is your parents, your siblings, your partner, your boss, or even just the saleslady in the department store, all people around you deserve to be respected. If you do not want them to end up disrespecting you or putting aside your feelings, then, you need to start showing them that you also deserve to be respected. How do you do it? You respect them first.

Aside from respect being a two-way communication, love also takes on the same path. As the old adage goes, it takes two to tango. You can never expect other people to love you when the only thing that you show them is disgust and hate.

But when you say love other people, it does not necessarily mean that you need to be sending them flowers, chocolates, and I Love You notes every now and then. Love is not only about those things. Love is more than what the material things can do. It is something that is naturally embedded in every person's heart and it comes out every time they do things that are not only for their own sake but also for those around them. Love is a little child that gives his half of bread to a classmate who did not have anything for lunch. Love is a lady who helped a grandmother carry her bag of groceries and ensure that she safely rides a taxi. Love is when an older brother helps his younger sister to build her doll house. You see, even the simplest things that you do every day can already be a way of showing love, it is just that you might not be aware of it because you are too focused on the kind of love that you see in romantic movies.

By learning to treat other people with love and respect, you are also giving yourself a chance of receiving the same love and respect from them in return. Who wouldn't want to be respected and loved anyway? For sure, you want to feel these things too and the best way for you to achieve this is by learning to treat those people around you, and that means not only your family and friends, but also others, with the same level of respect and love that you want for yourself.

CHAPTER 3

BEING GRATEFUL

Synopsis

Is being grateful part of your daily routine? Do you say "Thank You" for even the simplest things that you receive? If not, then, it is never too late for you to finally realize the essence of being grateful for all the things in your life after you have read this chapter.

The True Essence of Being Grateful

Whether you feel angry, moody, jealous or depressed recently or you feel that your life is full of negativities at this very moment, it is really never too late for you to enjoy the numerous benefits that being grateful has to offer.

In fact, you can take a few minutes any time and be thankful for the things that exist in your life, good or bad, happy or sad, for these can all make you grow into the kind of person that you are.

Seeing through the bad times and still being thankful might not really be easy but after you have surpassed them and you look back at your life's darkest moments, you will surely appreciate the thing that you got from it = a tougher skin, a useful lesson or even just the mere experience which can help you in making better choices in the near future.

So, what are the benefits that you can get when you are grateful?

- This helps you to be in the present, allowing you to notice the things that you have and stopping in order to acknowledge all of them. It can be as simple as having a pizza for lunch, the company of a classmate, or even the ability to hear.

- Being grateful can generate good vibes. When applied to positive thinking, quantum physics state that your thoughts' vibration can modify and affect the reality that surrounds you. It has been said that the initial 17 seconds of your thoughts are the most powerful, creating sufficient energy needed for starting attracting the things you are thinking of to come to your life.

- When you are grateful, you have the power to change your mood almost immediately from negative into positive. Positive energy and good feelings arise once you start to acknowledge the things you are thankful for.

However, there are some instances when your negative emotions start ruling you and affecting your mood. During these cases, it can be a bit hard for you to be actually grateful for anything.

When this situation befalls you, just think of this thought: things can always be much worst.

Whatever kind of circumstances you might be in, there is a chance that these can become way more difficult than what you are in right now. Be thankful that you are not in that "worst" part and try looking at things in a more positive light.

For instance, your budget probably doesn't allow you to get a new pair of shoes but still, you have 5 other pairs when the other girl in your class doesn't even have one.

You will finally be able to see the true essence of being grateful once you come to the realization that you can actually use your thankful feelings to achieve the things that you want. Be thankful today and expect for more blessings tomorrow.

CHAPTER 4

EXPRESSING YOURSELF

Synopsis

Expressing yourself is more than just saying words out loud. One important key to being disciplined enough is knowing what and how to say things in such a way that it will not negatively affect other people around you. In this chapter, you will get to learn the right ways of expressing yourself.

Tips to Help You Express Yourself Properly

Whether you are at your home, the office or a social event, the most crucial thing that matters a lot is how you express your feelings and your thoughts. Simply put, it is your body language combined with your attitude that matters. Aside from that, it is also about you can confidently present yourself in front of others.

Your personality will always project your perception that is why it is a must for you to present yourself in such a way that other people will not make out wrong things about you. This does not necessarily mean that you have to change your personality. Instead, just a little polishing will already be able to help you in overcoming the loop holes. So, what are the things that you can try to groom yourself and gain that confidence when expressing yourself?

The first and definitely the most important thing that you need to check is your attitude. A sense of individuality is something that you need to have all the time. If you want to befriend someone, being defensive is a big no-no.

Keep a welcoming and warm future, giving them the best from your end.

See to it that when you speak, you sound assertive, only not too much because when you overdo it and sound more intense than what is necessary, you can end up sounding aggressive to. If you have something to say, say it properly coupled with the right amount of confidence right from the get go.

Always remember one rule when you want to express yourself: it is not just about the things that you say but also how you say them, which means that you have to make it a point that you always put things forward in such a way that you will not hurt other people's feelings.

You also have to pay attention to your voice's pitch. Being too harsh and too soft will not do the trick. Get your voice properly modulated for it to sound right and will reflect your confidence.

The next time that you feel like expressing yourself, it is important for you to remember these tips that can help a lot for you to leave the person/persons with a good impression of you as someone with a pleasing and confident personality.

CHAPTER 5

GET OUT OF THE PAST

Synopsis

They say that moving on is never easy. Forgetting the past is not as simple as taking off your shoes to change to your slippers. However, getting out of the past becomes of great importance if you want your future to be better and not something that is being run by the things that have already happened and things that you can no longer change. In this chapter, discover the true importance of learning the art of letting go.

Let Bygones Be Bygones – Forget But Learn From The Past

Humans by nature tend to hold to an event that made them feel hurt or disappointed. Whether it just happened yesterday or 40 years ago, there are some wounds that remain deep and difficult to heal. However, life goes on and sometimes, you need to start with the healing process if you want your life to become even better, or even happier.

Grudges, anger, hurt, disappointment and other negative things that you have felt in the past shouldn't be allowed to dwell in your present. Granted that these are important and still a part of molding you into the person that you are right now, you must not let the past to control you and the decisions that you make at present and in the future.

Since everyone is different, it is only understandable for them to have different and unique ways of handling certain situations. However, there is no point to dwelling on the "what ifs" and "could have beens." What if I did this? It could have been like this if I did that. No matter what answers or questions you make, still, it will never make your present. Mulling the past over and over in your mind will only add to your current problems and worse, these can even bring about even more issues that you have to deal with.

When you get hurt, you can feel devastated and there are even times when your hurt can turn to anger, and anger becomes bitterness and this bitterness ignites the unwillingness to forgive. Living without forgiving can damage your emotional, physical, mental, as well as spiritual health. It is the very reason why you need to get out of your past and forgive the ones that hurt you because this is the only way for you to prevent the other aspects of your life from suffering as well.

And when you say get out of the past and forgive the persons that hurt you, you also need to remember that you also need to learn forgiving yourself at the same time. Everyone has things that they struggle with and no one in this world is perfect and free from flaws. While it is true that you have probably made a mistake in the past, still, you have to learn forgiving yourself for the part that you had in that particular situation. Nursing and holding on to your guilt will never do you any good, and will only restrict you from your chances of enjoying and living your life to the fullest.

All kinds of relationships can end in as quickly as they started, a fact that you have to accept. But even with this, you should always bear in your mind that no matter what happens, the tunnel will always have a light on its end. You can always get out of the past, forget the situation that brought devastations to your life. And for you to do that, you need to have the willingness of doing your past and choose to leave your past behind.

CHAPTER 6

MANAGE MATERIAL OBJECTS

Synopsis

Do you consider your material possessions as the best things that you have in this world? Are the objects in your life all that matters to you? If yes, then, you have to realize that you need to know the right ways of properly managing your material objects.

Life is Valuable – Don't Waste It Chasing Possessions

You can become happier when you pursue less instead of pursuing more. For some, this might not be the case but for others, they will surely agree that this is definitely true.

But the problem is, right from the day that you were born into this world, you have been told of something different – that more material objects mean more joys. And since this is a message that you heard a lot of times coming from different angles, you actually started believing. This is the very reason why a lot of people work long hours just to earn money and buy nice things.

However, the moment that you hear the message that more joy awaits you when you pursue less compared to when you pursue more, deep in your heart, you know that this is true. Material objects do not equal joy and you know that your life is way more valuable to just waste it chasing these things.

You only get one shot at life so as much as possible, make the most out of your limited time on this earth by managing the things that you own. While there is nothing wrong to dream of having your own laptop, a smartphone, a tablet or a car, you still have to know that these material things are not your only source of happiness and fulfillment. Use them as they are meant to be used but do not go to the extent that they become the whole world to you and you end up forgetting the things and the people that matter the most in your life.

Always remember that happiness, joy and fulfillment are things that can be found in life's invisible things: relationships, hope, peace, and love. You cannot find these things offered on sale at the department store in your area nor can you buy them in discounted prices.

If you already have a smartphone or a tablet, be contented with it and don't overwork yourself just so you can get more. When you do so, you will only end up wanting more because at the end of the day, these material objects will never be able to satisfy the deepest desires of your heart.

As you wake up every morning, remind yourself that your life is too precious to just waste it going after material objects. If you want real joy, choose to go for "better," not "more."

CHAPTER 7

JOURNALING

Synopsis

Did you ever try keeping a personal journal? If this idea is new to you, then, you will surely be more motivated to keep one once you have finished this chapter and learn the wonderful benefits that journaling has to offer.

The Perks of Keeping Your Own Journal or Diary

For hundreds of years, journaling has already been around and a staple part of the lives of the people from different countries. In fact, it was through the personal diaries that information regarding governments and countries was discovered, together with the people that lived during certain time periods. Today, journaling has become a way for people not just to express themselves but also to learn more about themselves. By keeping your own journal, you are also going to experience a lot of benefits, especially when you write it on a regular basis.

For starters, journaling will help you in clarifying your goals in life aside from allowing you to write down your ideas and achievements. With your journal, you can clearly see the steps that you take towards reaching your goal while simultaneously giving you the chance of seeing the exact point where you stand and how much further you still need to go for your goals to be completed.

Journaling can also help in making your life simple. Many people tend to make their lives more complicated than what it needs to be. There are a gazillion of things that have to be completed every day but if you will take some time to sit down and write on your journal, you will be amazed how you will start seeing the things that really matter in your life. Write down in your journal the values that you believe in and think of things that you are thankful for in your life.

Journals also have this amazing power of making you express what you feel about your relationships and your life as a whole. By keeping a journal, you can have that private place where you can vent out the frustrations that you have with your relationships. Journaling gives you the chance of realizing why

29

you feel bothered by a person's certain aspects and how you can change the way that you handle specific situations. Your journal will teach you how to love with more conviction and power that can make your relationships clearer and definitely much stronger.

The last but definitely not the least, journaling allows you to get to learn yourself even better. You can discus about your values, morals as well as other beliefs. Through this, you can clarify your own stand on particular topics and at the same time, you can also express yourself in a clearer manner. If someone happens to ask you about one controversy or topic and what your thoughts about it are, it will be easier for you to lay down your opinion in just several seconds, which will then make you as someone who knows yourself well in the eyes of other persons.

CHAPTER 8

BEING PERSISTENT

Synopsis

Was there ever a time when you simply refused to go on just because you failed once? Did your feelings ever interfere with the decisions that you make in your life? Are you someone who easily surrenders after just a single mistake? Well, you probably lack persistence if you answer all these questions with a yes. Being persistent is a must in this game of life and in this chapter, you will get to know more about this much needed trait that you should start to develop.

Persistence and Its True Value

Persistence refers to a person's ability of continuously moving forward whatever your feelings might be. Persistence is when you push on just when you feel like you want to throw up your hands, surrender and quit altogether. Persistence is the combination of desire and will power, the urge to get there, no matter what happens. Being persistent is having steel determination.

Imagine how your life is going to be if you are persistent enough to do, be and have all the things that you want. Well, this can sound a bit farfetched but it surely fun to try.

Whether they admit it or not, there are simply a lot of people who easily give up at first sign of opposition and adversity and only a selected few choose to go on until they reached their goals.

Being persistent is not something that you get from holding on to the past. Instead, it comes from the vision that you get of your future. It is important to keep that burning desire in you for this vision to be real, pushing you to give everything just so it can be possible.

Once you start with a certain task, things may move rather slowly but if you are persistent, you can accomplish the job and move on to the next step.

Every accomplishment you make will build up on one another, with you becoming an expert every step of the way.

Persistence and its value stems from keeping your eyes on your target, even when you reached the lowest low and when the whole world seems to go against you. Persistence is when you still manage to stand up and face the challenges.

CHAPTER 9

DON'T DEFINE YOURSELF BY MISTAKES

Synopsis

There is no need for you to live a life full of shame and regret and guilt. You must never make your mistakes define you. You are more than that poor response, that bad choice, that one rebellious moment than all or any of the mistakes and failures that you had – present, past, or in the future.

You are Not Your Mistakes

As a human, you are always bound to make mistakes – whether in your personal life, your marriage, your work, your family. Everyone will make mistake, a wrong choice at a certain point in your life. All mistakes that you make should be the source of your strength. These mistakes must be the lessons that you learn in your life. Grow from them. Be better because of

34

them. Make the necessary amendments and continue with your life. You should not cling or dwell on your mistakes for the rest of your remaining years on this earth.

All people have a path to follow. All people have choices that decide the path where they should go down. Once you make a mistake, just say sorry. Fix your mistake if possible and vow that you will do better in the future. It will help change the path you are taking, giving you the chance to become a better person.

Use your mistakes not just for making yourself better but also for teaching your children and other people around you to avoid making a similar mistake.

It is completely shameful to hold your mistakes over others, use it against them or blackmail them. Every now and then, you will make mistakes and holding it over another person's head is yet another mistake. In the same way that God forgives, everyone should too. You have to let go of things.

You have to let people amend or change their mistakes, turn things into a better direction and not continuously beat them up for them.

Never allow your mistakes to pull you down. Don't define yourself by the mistakes that you made. Keep your head up. Pick yourself up. Acknowledge the wrongs that you have done. Learn from the mistakes you made and become a better version of yourself. Give the people around you with the same benefit of the doubt and understand that just like you, they also make mistakes but just like you, they can also get past these things.

Forgiveness is always the key. Forgive others. Forgive yourself. Move on.

CHAPTER 10

BENEFITS OF KNOWING
WHAT DESERVES ATTENTION

Synopsis

While living in this wide world can be too overwhelming, with a lot of things demanding for your attention, you should realize that not all of the things that you see, the things that you hear, the things that you feel, require you interest. There are some things that need to be let go of, some things that you simply need to forget, things that you simply have to let be. There are benefits that you can enjoy once you learned knowing what really deserves your attention and in this last chapter, expect to become better, an updated version of you.

Focus Your Attention On Those That Really Matter

People by nature want to live the best life that they can ever have, a life where everything is balanced, a life that is free from regrets, a life that is perfect.

However, if there is one important thing that you have to always remember, it is the fact that there is no such thing as a perfect life. That every now and then, you will fall. Every now and then, darkness will envelop your life.

Every now and then, life is not what you dream it to be.

Since life isn't always as you see it, it is important for you to start focusing your attention only on those that truly deserve. While you will feel that you have to give your attention to everything around you, you need to keep in mind that there are just some things that you do not have control with.

There are people, things, and events that you simply have to let go of and let be.

By learning how to identify the things that truly deserve your attention, you will come to see that you can manage your life better. Your life will also become much easier and bearable because you no longer linger on those that do not matter. Whether it is a mistake, a failure, a person that chose a different path, a path away from yours, letting go of them will change the overall state of your life.

If you can identify right away the things that really deserve your full attention, you will be able to know your priorities. You will know what must be included at the top of the list, and those that you should worry about the least. When your priorities are set properly, it will be easier for you to meet all of them. You will not have a hard time choosing what should be done first because you know exactly where you are going and how you will go there. Setting your priorities in place makes your life more manageable and you are also ensured that your attention is divided equally.

When you know what deserves your attention, you can expect a better life ahead of you. Yes, it may not be perfect and mistakes and failures will always be there every now and then. But what matters most is that you still live the life exactly how you want to live it, a life that you can be proud of.

Printed by Libri Plureos GmbH in Hamburg, Germany